THE MENOPAUSE DIE

Delicious Recipes to Improve Your Shape and Feel Great Again

By logan short

Copyright © 2023 Logan short

All rights reserved. No part of this book may be reproduced, stored in a retrieval system, or transmitted, in any form or by any means, electronic, mechanical, photocopying, recording, or otherwise, without the prior written permission of the publisher.

This book is a work of non-fiction. While every effort has been made to ensure the accuracy of the information contained within, the author and publisher cannot accept responsibility for any errors or omissions that may occur.

TABLE OF CONTENTS

INTRODUCTION 5
The Menopause Phase: What is it? 11
The Importance of a Healthy Diet During Menopause 14
CHAPTER ONE 19
Understanding the Menopause Diet 19
The Basics of a Menopause-Friendly Diet 21
Essential Nutrients for Menopause 23
Foods to Avoid During Menopause 25
CHAPTER TWO 27
Creating a Meal Plan for Menopause 27
Designing a Balanced Meal Plan for Menopause 29
Sample meal plan for menopause: 31
Tips for managing menopause symptoms through diet: 33
Sample Meal Plans for Menopause 34
Meal Plan 1: 34
Meal Plan 2: 36
Meal Plan 3: 38
Menopause-Friendly Recipes 40
Recipe 1 40

Recipe 2 41

Recipe 3: 43

CHAPTER THREE 45

Superfoods for 45

Benefits of Superfoods for Menopause 47

CHAPTER FOUR 55

Exercise for Menopause 55

Stress Management for Menopause 58

Sleep Hygiene for Menopause 62

Chapter five 69

Menopause Supplements and Medications 69

Other Medications for Menopause Symptoms 73

CHAPTER SIX 75

Managing Menopause Symptoms Naturally 75

Acupuncture for Menopause Symptoms 78

Other Natural Approaches to Menopause Symptoms 79

CONCLUSION 83

The Importance of a Menopause Diet Plan 83

Tips for Successful Menopause Management 85

Embracing Menopause as a New Chapter in Your Life. ... 87

INTRODUCTION

As women age, they experience a number of changes in their bodies, including the transition through menopause. Menopause is a natural biological process that marks the end of a woman's reproductive years.

It is a time when estrogen and progesterone levels decline, which can lead to a number of physical and emotional symptoms, including hot flashes, night sweats, mood swings, and vaginal dryness.

While menopause is a natural part of the aging process, it can be challenging for many women. However, making certain dietary changes can help alleviate some of the symptoms associated with menopause and support overall health and well-being.

The menopause diet plan is designed to provide women with a range of foods that can help alleviate the symptoms of menopause, support bone health, and improve overall health and well-being.

This diet plan focuses on whole, nutrient-dense foods that provide essential vitamins, minerals, and nutrients, while avoiding processed and sugary foods that can increase inflammation in the body and contribute to weight gain.

One of the key principles of the menopause diet plan is to prioritize foods that are high in phytoestrogens. Phytoestrogens are plant-based compounds that can mimic the effects of estrogen in the body.

During menopause, estrogen levels decline, which can contribute to a range of symptoms. Incorporating foods that are high in phytoestrogens, such as soy products, flaxseeds, lentils, and chickpeas, can help alleviate some of the symptoms associated with menopause.

Another important principle of the menopause diet plan is to increase calcium and vitamin D intake. Women going through menopause are at an increased risk of osteoporosis, which is a condition that weakens bones and increases the risk of fractures.

Adequate calcium and vitamin D intake can help support bone health and reduce the risk of osteoporosis. Foods that are high in calcium and vitamin D include dairy products, leafy greens, and fortified foods.

In addition to incorporating specific foods into the diet, the menopause diet plan also emphasizes the importance of staying hydrated.

Hormonal changes during menopause can lead to increased dehydration, so it is important to drink plenty of water and other hydrating fluids throughout the day. Staying hydrated can help support healthy skin, digestion, and overall health.

The menopause diet plan also recommends avoiding processed and sugary foods. These foods can increase inflammation in the body and contribute to weight gain, which can exacerbate symptoms of menopause such as hot flashes and mood swings.

Instead, the diet plan recommends focusing on whole, nutrient-dense foods that provide adequate nutrition and support overall health and well-being.

Overall, the menopause diet plan is designed to provide women with a range of foods that can help alleviate the symptoms of menopause and support overall health and well-being. By incorporating specific foods into the diet and avoiding others, women can support bone health, reduce inflammation in the body, and alleviate symptoms such as hot flashes and mood swings.

Is women age, they experience a number of changes in their bodies, including the transition through menopause. Menopause is a natural biological process that marks the end of a woman's reproductive years.

It is a time when estrogen and progesterone levels decline, which can lead to a number of physical and emotional symptoms, including hot flashes, night sweats, mood swings, and vaginal dryness.

While menopause is a natural part of the aging process, it can be challenging for many women. However, making certain dietary changes can help alleviate some of the symptoms associated with menopause and support overall health and well-being.

The menopause diet plan is designed to provide women with a range of foods that can help alleviate the symptoms of menopause, support bone health, and improve overall health and well-being. This diet plan focuses on whole, nutrient-dense foods that provide essential vitamins, minerals, and nutrients, while avoiding processed and sugary foods that can increase inflammation in the body and contribute to weight gain.

One of the key principles of the menopause diet plan is to prioritize foods that are high in phytoestrogens. Phytoestrogens are plant-based compounds that can mimic the effects of estrogen in the body.

During menopause, estrogen levels decline, which can contribute to a range of symptoms. Incorporating foods that are high in phytoestrogens, such as soy products, flaxseeds, lentils, and chickpeas, can help alleviate some of the symptoms associated with menopause.

Another important principle of the menopause diet plan is to increase calcium and vitamin D intake. Women going through menopause are at an increased risk of osteoporosis, which is a condition that weakens bones and increases the risk of fractures.

Adequate calcium and vitamin D intake can help support bone health and reduce the risk of osteoporosis. Foods that are high in calcium and vitamin D include dairy products, leafy greens, and fortified foods.

In addition to incorporating specific foods into the diet, the menopause diet plan also emphasizes the importance of staying hydrated. Hormonal changes during menopause can lead to increased dehydration, so it is important to drink plenty of water and other hydrating fluids throughout the day. Staying hydrated can help support healthy skin, digestion, and overall health.

The menopause diet plan also recommends avoiding processed and sugary foods. These foods can increase inflammation in the body and contribute to weight gain, which can exacerbate symptoms of menopause such as hot flashes and mood swings.

Instead, the diet plan recommends focusing on whole, nutrient-dense foods that provide adequate nutrition and support overall health and well-being.

Overall, the menopause diet plan is designed to provide women with a range of foods that can help alleviate the symptoms of menopause and support overall health and well-being. By incorporating specific foods into the diet and avoiding others, women can support bone health, reduce inflammation in the body, and alleviate symptoms such as hot flashes and mood swings.

The Menopause Phase: What is it?

Menopause is a natural biological process that marks the end of a woman's reproductive years. It is a phase that typically occurs in women between the ages of 45 and 55, with the average age of onset being 51.

Menopause is defined as the absence of menstrual periods for 12 months, and it signals the end of fertility. While menopause is a normal part of the aging process, it can bring about a variety of physical and emotional changes in a woman's life.

During menopause, the ovaries stop producing eggs, and the levels of estrogen and progesterone hormones decrease. These hormonal changes can lead to a variety of symptoms, including hot flashes, night sweats, vaginal dryness, mood swings, and difficulty sleeping.

Some women may also experience other symptoms such as weight gain, joint pain, and dry skin. While these symptoms can be distressing, they are a natural part of the menopause process and can be managed with lifestyle changes or medical treatments.

There are three stages of menopause: perimenopause, menopause, and post menopause. Perimenopause is the stage that precedes menopause and can begin several years before a woman's final menstrual period.

During perimenopause, hormone levels start to fluctuate, and women may experience irregular periods, hot flashes, and other symptoms. Menopause is the stage that occurs when a woman has gone 12 months without a menstrual period.

Post menopause is the stage that follows menopause and lasts for the rest of a woman's life. During this stage, menopause symptoms may continue, and women may be at increased risk for certain health conditions such as osteoporosis and heart disease.

While menopause is a natural part of the aging process, it can have a significant impact on a woman's physical and emotional health. Women going through menopause may experience a range of emotions, including sadness, anxiety, and depression. It's important for women to talk to their healthcare provider about any physical or emotional changes they are experiencing during this time. They can help provide guidance on managing symptoms and offer support for emotional health.

Treatment options for menopause symptoms vary depending on the individual and the severity of their symptoms. Hormone replacement therapy (HRT) is a common treatment option that can help alleviate hot flashes, night sweats, and other symptoms.

However, HRT may increase the risk of certain health conditions such as breast cancer, blood clots, and stroke. Women should discuss the risks and benefits of HRT with their healthcare provider to determine if it is the right treatment option for them.

Other treatment options for menopause symptoms include lifestyle changes such as regular exercise, a healthy diet, and stress reduction techniques like yoga or meditation. Over-the-counter remedies such as black cohosh and soy supplements may also help alleviate menopause symptoms.

Women should talk to their healthcare provider before starting any new treatments to ensure they are safe and effective.

In conclusion, menopause is a natural biological process that marks the end of a woman's reproductive years. While it can bring about physical and emotional changes, there are many treatment options available to help manage symptoms and improve overall health.

Women should talk to their healthcare provider about any concerns they have regarding menopause and work together to develop a plan that meets their individual needs.

The Importance of a Healthy Diet During Menopause

Menopause is a natural biological process that marks the end of a woman's reproductive years. It can bring about a variety of physical and emotional changes, including weight gain, hot flashes, mood swings, and difficulty sleeping. While menopause is a normal part of the aging process, it is important for women to maintain a healthy diet during this time to manage symptoms and reduce the risk of certain health conditions.

A healthy diet during menopause should include a variety of nutrient-dense foods that provide the necessary vitamins, minerals, and other nutrients to support overall health.

This can include whole grains, fruits, vegetables, lean protein sources, and healthy fats. The following are some reasons why a healthy diet is important during menopause:

1. **Helps manage weight gain**: Many women experience weight gains during menopause due to hormonal changes and a decrease in physical activity.

A healthy diet that includes plenty of fruits, vegetables, and whole grains can help women maintain a healthy weight and reduce the risk of obesity-related health conditions such as diabetes, heart disease, and high blood pressure.

2. **Supports bone health**: Women are at increased risk for osteoporosis during and after menopause due to a decrease in estrogen levels.

A healthy diet that includes calcium-rich foods such as dairy products, leafy green vegetables, and fortified foods can help support bone health and reduce the risk of fractures.

3. **Reduces the risk of heart disease**: Women's risk for heart disease increases after menopause due to changes in hormone levels. A healthy diet that includes plenty of fruits, vegetables, whole grains, and healthy fats can help reduce the risk of heart disease by lowering cholesterol levels, reducing inflammation, and improving blood pressure.

4. **Improves mood and sleep**: Menopause can bring about mood swings and difficulty sleeping. A healthy diet that includes complex carbohydrates such as whole grains and fruits can help stabilize blood sugar levels and improve mood and sleep.

5. **Reduces hot flashes**: Some women experience hot flashes during menopause, which can be uncomfortable and disruptive. A healthy diet that includes phytoestrogens, such as soy products and flaxseed, may help reduce the frequency and intensity of hot flashes.

It is important for women to focus on nutrient-dense foods during menopause and avoid foods that can worsen symptoms, such as alcohol, caffeine, and spicy foods. Women should also aim to stay hydrated by drinking plenty of water and avoiding sugary drinks.

In addition to a healthy diet, women can also benefit from regular exercise and stress-reduction techniques such as yoga or meditation. Exercise can help maintain a healthy weight, improve bone health, and reduce the risk of heart disease. Stress-reduction techniques can help improve mood and sleep and reduce the frequency and intensity of hot flashes.

In conclusion, a healthy diet is an important part of managing menopause symptoms and reducing the risk of certain health conditions. Women should focus on nutrient-dense foods and avoid foods that can worsen symptoms. In addition, regular exercise and stress-reduction techniques can also help improve overall health and well-being during menopause.

It is important for women to talk to their healthcare provider about any concerns they have regarding menopause and work together to develop a plan that meets their individual needs.

CHAPTER ONE

Understanding the Menopause Diet

Menopause is a natural biological process that occurs in women as they age. It marks the end of the menstrual cycle and is usually diagnosed when a woman has gone without a period for 12 consecutive months.

Menopause brings about a variety of physical and emotional changes in women, including hot flashes, night sweats, mood swings, weight gain, and decreased bone density.

While there is no one-size-fits-all solution for managing menopause symptoms, a healthy diet can play a significant role in helping women navigate this transition. The menopause diet involves consuming a balanced, nutrient-dense diet that includes plenty of whole foods and minimizes processed foods and added sugars.

Here are some key elements of the menopause diet:

1. **Phytoestrogens:** These are plant compounds that mimic the effects of estrogen in the body. Foods rich

in phytoestrogens include soybeans, tofu, flaxseeds, lentils, chickpeas, and red clover.

2. **Calcium and Vitamin D:** These nutrients are crucial for maintaining bone health, which can decline during menopause. Good sources of calcium include dairy products, leafy green vegetables, and fortified foods. Vitamin D is primarily obtained through exposure to sunlight, but can also be found in fatty fish and fortified foods.

3. **Omega-3 Fatty Acids**: These healthy fats can help reduce inflammation in the body and support brain health. Good sources of omega-3s include fatty fish, nuts and seeds, and plant oils.

4. **Fiber**: Eating a high-fiber diet can help regulate digestion, maintain healthy cholesterol levels, and reduce the risk of certain diseases. Good sources of fiber include whole grains, fruits, vegetables, and legumes.

Water: Staying hydrated is important for overall health, especially during menopause when hot flashes and night sweats can cause excessive sweating. Aim to drink at least 8 cups of water per day.

By incorporating these elements into your diet, you can help alleviate some of the uncomfortable symptoms of menopause and promote overall health.

The Basics of a Menopause-Friendly Diet

A menopause-friendly diet should focus on consuming a variety of whole, nutrient-dense foods while minimizing processed foods, added sugars, and saturated and trans fats. Here are some key principles to keep in mind:

1. **Focus on Whole Foods**: Whole foods are those that are minimally processed and contain a variety of essential nutrients. Examples include fruits, vegetables, whole grains, lean protein, and healthy fats.

2. **Prioritize Protein:** Protein is important for maintaining muscle mass and bone health during menopause. Choose lean sources of protein such as fish, poultry, beans, nuts, and seeds.

3. **Eat Plenty of Fruits and Vegetables:** Fruits and vegetables are rich in vitamins, minerals, fiber, and antioxidants, which can help reduce inflammation and support overall health. Aim to eat at least five servings per day.
4. **Choose Healthy Fats**: Healthy fats such as those found in nuts, seeds, avocados, and olive oil can help reduce inflammation and support brain health. Avoid foods high in saturated and trans fats such as fried foods, processed snacks, and fatty meats.
5. **Limit Added Sugars**: Too much added sugar can contribute to weight gain, inflammation, and other health issues. Read labels carefully and limit foods high in added sugars such as candy, soda, and baked goods.
6. **Stay Hydrated:** Drinking plenty of water can help alleviate symptoms of menopause such as hot flashes and night sweats. Aim to drink at least 8 cups of water per day.

By following these guidelines, you can create a menopause-friendly diet that supports your overall health and helps manage menopause symptoms.

Essential Nutrients for Menopause

Menopause is a natural transition that brings about changes in a woman's body, including a decrease in estrogen levels, which can lead to symptoms such as hot flashes, mood swings, and bone loss. Eating a nutrient-dense diet that provides essential nutrients can help support overall health and alleviate some of these symptoms.

Here are some essential nutrients to consider:

1. **Calcium**: Calcium is essential for maintaining bone health and preventing osteoporosis, a condition that causes bones to become weak and brittle. Good sources of calcium include dairy products, leafy green vegetables, and fortified foods.

2. **Vitamin D**: Vitamin D helps the body absorb calcium and is important for maintaining bone health. The best source of vitamin D is exposure to sunlight, but it can also be found in fatty fish and fortified foods.

3. **Magnesium**: Magnesium plays a role in maintaining bone health, regulating blood sugar, and supporting nerve and muscle function. Good sources of magnesium include nuts, seeds, whole grains, and leafy green vegetables.
4. **Omega-3 Fatty Acids**: Omega-3 fatty acids are healthy fats that can help reduce inflammation and support brain health. Good sources of omega-3s include fatty fish, nuts and seeds, and plant oils.
5. **Phytoestrogens:** Phytoestrogens are plant compounds that mimic the effects of estrogen in the body. Foods rich in phytoestrogens include soybeans, tofu, flaxseeds, lentils, chickpeas, and red clover.
6. **B Vitamins**: B vitamins are important for energy metabolism, nerve function, and healthy skin, hair, and nails. Good sources of B vitamins include whole grains, leafy green vegetables, and fortified foods.
7. **Iron**: Iron is important for maintaining healthy blood cells and preventing anemia, a condition that can cause fatigue and weakness. Good sources of iron

include lean meat, poultry, fish, beans, and fortified cereals.

By incorporating these essential nutrients into your diet, you can help support overall health and manage some of the symptoms of menopause.

Foods to Avoid During Menopause

During menopause, women experience a decrease in the production of the hormone estrogen, which can lead to a variety of symptoms. While there are no specific foods that women should avoid during menopause, there are certain foods that can exacerbate symptoms and make them feel worse. Here are some foods that women may want to limit or avoid during menopause:

1. **Caffeine**: Caffeine can increase hot flashes, anxiety, and insomnia, which are common symptoms of menopause.
2. **Alcohol**: Alcohol can trigger hot flashes, increase irritability, and disrupt sleep, which can make menopausal symptoms worse.

3. **Spicy foods:** Spicy foods can cause hot flashes and night sweats, which are already common symptoms of menopause.
4. **Sugar**: High sugar intake can worsen mood swings and hot flashes, and can also lead to weight gain, which can increase the risk of other health problems.
5. **Processed foods:** Processed foods are often high in salt and preservatives, which can lead to water retention and bloating, as well as exacerbate other menopausal symptoms.
6. **Red meat**: Red meat can increase inflammation in the body, which can worsen hot flashes and other menopausal symptoms.
7. **Dairy:** Some women find that dairy products, particularly milk, can trigger hot flashes and night sweats.

It's important to note that not all women experience the same symptoms during menopause, and some may find that they can still eat some of these foods without any issues. It's also important to maintain a balanced diet and to speak with a healthcare professional before making any major dietary changes.

CHAPTER TWO

Creating a Meal Plan for Menopause

Menopause is a significant hormonal shift in a woman's life, and it can lead to a variety of symptoms such as hot flashes, mood changes, and weight gain. To manage these symptoms, it is important to maintain a healthy diet that includes a balance of protein, carbohydrates, healthy fats, and essential vitamins and minerals.

Here is a sample meal plan for menopause:

1. Breakfast:

Oatmeal with nuts, berries, and almond milk

Greek yogurt with fruit and granola

Scrambled eggs with spinach and whole-grain toast

2. Mid-morning snack:

Apple slices with almond butter

Raw vegetables with hummus

Hard-boiled egg

3. **Lunch:**

Grilled chicken breast with quinoa and roasted vegetables

Turkey and avocado wrap with a side salad

Lentil soup with a whole-grain roll

4. **Afternoon snack:**

Trail mix with nuts, seeds, and dried fruit

Greek yogurt with honey and berries

Smoothie made with frozen fruit and almond milk

5. **Dinner:**

Baked salmon with brown rice and steamed broccoli

Grilled tofu with mixed greens and quinoa

Chicken stir-fry with vegetables and brown rice

6. **Evening snack:**

Dark chocolate

Popcorn with nutritional yeast

Low-sugar fruit such as berries or a small apple

In addition to these meal ideas, it is important to stay hydrated by drinking plenty of water throughout the day. You may also want to limit your intake of caffeine and alcohol, as these can exacerbate symptoms like hot flashes and mood swings.

Regular exercise and stress-reduction techniques like yoga or meditation can also help manage menopause symptoms.

Designing a Balanced Meal Plan for Menopause

Menopause is a natural process that marks the end of a woman's reproductive years. During this time, hormonal changes can lead to various symptoms such as hot flashes, mood swings, and weight gain. A balanced meal plan can help manage these symptoms and maintain overall health and well-being.

The following guidelines can help design a balanced meal plan for menopause:

1. Eat a variety of foods

Eating a variety of foods ensures that you get all the essential nutrients that your body needs. Include fruits, vegetables, whole grains, lean proteins, and healthy fats in your diet.

2. Focus on whole grains

Whole grains are a great source of fiber, which can help manage weight and reduce the risk of heart disease. Choose whole-grain bread, pasta, rice, and cereals over refined grains.

3. Include lean proteins

Protein is essential for building and repairing tissues in the body. Choose lean proteins like chicken, turkey, fish, beans, and legumes.

4. Eat healthy fats

Healthy fats, such as those found in avocados, nuts, seeds, and fatty fish like salmon, can help reduce inflammation and improve heart health.

5. Limit processed foods

Processed foods are often high in added sugars, salt, and unhealthy fats. They also lack essential nutrients. Limit your intake of processed foods and choose whole, minimally processed foods instead.

6. Stay hydrated

Drink plenty of water throughout the day to stay hydrated. You can also include other fluids like herbal tea, coconut water, and low-fat milk.

Sample meal plan for menopause:

Breakfast:

Oatmeal with almond milk, berries, and chopped nuts

Greek yogurt with granola and sliced banana

Scrambled eggs with sautéed vegetables and whole-grain toast

Mid-morning snack:

Apple slices with almond butter

Raw vegetables with hummus

Low-fat cheese with whole-grain crackers

Lunch:

Grilled chicken breast with mixed greens, quinoa, and roasted vegetables

Turkey and avocado wrap with a side salad

Lentil soup with whole-grain bread

Afternoon snack:

Trail mix with nuts, seeds, and dried fruit

Greek yogurt with honey and berries

Smoothie made with frozen fruit and low-fat milk

Dinner:

Baked salmon with brown rice and steamed broccoli

Grilled tofu with mixed greens and quinoa

Chicken stir-fry with vegetables and brown rice

Evening snack:

Dark chocolate

Popcorn with nutritional yeast

Low-sugar fruit such as berries or a small apple

Tips for managing menopause symptoms through diet:

1. Eat calcium-rich foods

During menopause, women may experience a loss of bone density, which can increase the risk of osteoporosis. Eating calcium-rich foods like low-fat dairy products, leafy green vegetables, and fortified foods like tofu and orange juice can help maintain bone health.

2. Include phytoestrogens

Phytoestrogens are plant compounds that can mimic the effects of estrogen in the body. Include phytoestrogen-rich foods like soy products, flaxseed, and legumes in your diet to manage menopause symptoms.

3. **Avoid trigger foods**

Certain foods can trigger hot flashes and other menopause symptoms. Common trigger foods include spicy foods, caffeine, alcohol, and processed foods. Pay attention to how your body reacts to different foods and avoid those that trigger symptoms.

4. **Manage weight**

Weight gain is common during menopause due to hormonal changes and a slowing metabolism. Eating a balanced diet and staying active can help manage weight and reduce the risk of chronic diseases like heart disease and diabetes.

Sample Meal Plans for Menopause

Here are three sample meal plans for menopause:

Meal Plan 1:

Breakfast:

Greek yogurt with berries, chopped nuts, and a drizzle of honey

Whole-grain toast with avocado and a hard-boiled egg

Oatmeal with almond milk, chopped apples, and cinnamon

Snack:

Baby carrots with hummus

Handful of almonds and dried cranberries

Low-fat string cheese and an apple

Lunch:

Grilled chicken salad with mixed greens, cherry tomatoes, sliced cucumber, and balsamic vinaigrette

Veggie wrap with roasted vegetables, hummus, and feta cheese

Quinoa bowl with black beans, avocado, salsa, and lime

Snack:

Greek yogurt with sliced banana and a sprinkle of cinnamon

Rice cake with almond butter and banana slices

Celery sticks with peanut butter

Dinner:

Baked salmon with lemon-dill sauce, brown rice, and steamed asparagus

Grilled tofu with quinoa and roasted vegetables

Baked chicken breast with sweet potato and mixed greens

Snack:

Dark chocolate

Air-popped popcorn with nutritional yeast

Frozen grapes

Meal Plan 2:

Breakfast:

Spinach and feta omelet with whole-grain toast

Smoothie with almond milk, frozen berries, and chia seeds

Low-fat cottage cheese with sliced peaches and whole-grain crackers

Snack:

Baby carrots with tzatziki sauce

Apple slices with almond butter

Hard-boiled egg

Lunch:

Grilled shrimp skewers with quinoa salad and mixed greens

Veggie burger with whole-grain bun, sweet potato fries, and side salad

Dinner:

Baked cod with lemon-herb sauce, brown rice, and roasted Brussels sprouts

Grilled portobello mushroom with quinoa and steamed green beans

Stir-fried chicken with vegetables and brown rice

Snack:

Low-fat cheese and whole-grain crackers

Air-popped popcorn with spices

Low-sugar fruit such as strawberries or blueberries

Meal Plan 3:

Breakfast:

Whole-grain waffle with almond butter and sliced banana

Scrambled eggs with spinach and whole-grain toast

Smoothie with low-fat milk, frozen fruit, and flaxseed

Snack:

Low-fat yogurt with chopped nuts and dried fruit

Rice cake with hummus and sliced cucumber

Apple slices with low-fat cheese

Lunch:

Grilled steak with mixed greens, roasted vegetables, and quinoa

Tuna salad with whole-grain crackers and side salad

Lentil soup with whole-grain bread

Snack:

Hard-boiled egg

Air-popped popcorn with herbs and spices

Sliced cucumber with tzatziki sauce

Dinner:

Baked chicken thighs with sweet potato and green beans

Grilled salmon with mixed greens and roasted vegetables

Vegetarian chili with brown rice

Snack:

Dark chocolate

Low-fat cottage cheese with sliced peaches

Frozen yogurt with berries

Menopause-Friendly Recipes

Here are three menopause-friendly recipes:

Recipe 1:

Kale and Quinoa Salad with Grilled Chicken

Ingredients:

1 bunch kale, chopped

1 cup cooked quinoa

1 red bell pepper, sliced

1 yellow bell pepper, sliced

1/2 red onion, sliced

1/4 cup feta cheese

2 boneless, skinless chicken breasts

1/4 cup olive oil

2 tablespoons balsamic vinegar

Salt and pepper, to taste

Directions:

Preheat grill to medium-high heat.

Brush chicken breasts with 2 tablespoons of olive oil and season with salt and pepper.

Grill chicken for 6-8 minutes per side, or until cooked through.

In a large bowl, combine kale, quinoa, peppers, and red onion.

In a small bowl, whisk together remaining olive oil, balsamic vinegar, salt, and pepper.

Pour dressing over salad and toss to coat.

Divide salad onto plates and top with sliced chicken and crumbled feta cheese.

Recipe 2:

Vegetarian Lentil Soup

Ingredients:

1 tablespoon olive oil

1 onion, chopped

2 cloves garlic, minced

1 teaspoon ground cumin

1 teaspoon ground coriander

1/2 teaspoon ground turmeric

4 cups vegetable broth

1 cup dried lentils, rinsed

1 can diced tomatoes

1/2 teaspoon salt

1/4 teaspoon black pepper

1/4 cup chopped fresh cilantro

Directions:

Heat olive oil in a large pot over medium heat.

Add onion and garlic, and sauté for 3-4 minutes, or until softened.

Stir in cumin, coriander, and turmeric and cook for 1-2 minutes.

Add vegetable broth, lentils, diced tomatoes, salt, and pepper to the pot.

Bring to a boil, then reduce heat to low and simmer for 30-40 minutes, or until lentils are tender.

Stir in cilantro and serve.

Recipe 3:

Grilled Salmon with Avocado Salsa

Ingredients:

4 salmon fillets

1 tablespoon olive oil

1 teaspoon chili powder

1 teaspoon cumin

Salt and pepper, to taste

2 avocados, diced

1/2 red onion, diced

1 red bell pepper, diced

Juice of 1 lime

1/4 cup chopped fresh cilantro

Directions:

Preheat grill to medium-high heat.

Brush salmon fillets with olive oil and season with chili powder, cumin, salt, and pepper.

Grill salmon for 4-5 minutes per side, or until cooked through.

In a bowl, combine diced avocado, red onion, red bell pepper, lime juice, cilantro, salt, and pepper.

Serve salmon fillets with avocado salsa on top.

CHAPTER THREE

Superfoods for

Menopause is a natural process that occurs in women when they reach a certain age. It is a time when a woman's body undergoes significant hormonal changes, which can lead to various physical and emotional symptoms. Eating a healthy, balanced diet is important during menopause to help manage these symptoms and maintain overall health. Here are some superfoods that can be particularly beneficial for women going through menopause:

1. **Soy products:** Soy products like tofu, soy milk, and edamame contain phytoestrogens, which are plant compounds that can mimic estrogen in the body. Consuming soy products may help relieve menopausal symptoms like hot flashes, night sweats, and mood swings.

2. **Flaxseeds:** Flaxseeds are high in lignans, which are phytoestrogens that may help regulate hormone levels in menopausal women. They are also a good

source of omega-3 fatty acids, which can help reduce inflammation and lower the risk of heart disease.

3. **Leafy greens**: Leafy greens like kale, spinach, and collard greens are rich in vitamins and minerals, including calcium, which is important for maintaining strong bones. They also contain antioxidants that can help reduce inflammation in the body.

4. **Berries:** Berries like blueberries, strawberries, and raspberries are high in antioxidants, which can help reduce oxidative stress in the body. They may also help improve cognitive function and reduce the risk of heart disease.

5. **Fatty fish**: Fatty fish like salmon, tuna, and sardines are rich in omega-3 fatty acids, which can help reduce inflammation and lower the risk of heart disease. They may also help improve mood and cognitive function.

6. **Nuts and seeds**: Nuts and seeds like almonds, walnuts, and pumpkin seeds are high in healthy fats, fiber, and protein. They can help reduce

inflammation in the body and may also help improve cognitive function.

7. **Whole grains**: Whole grains like quinoa, brown rice, and whole wheat bread are high in fiber, which can help regulate digestion and reduce the risk of heart disease. They are also a good source of vitamins and minerals, including magnesium, which may help reduce symptoms of menopause like anxiety and depression.

It is important to note that there is no one-size-fits-all approach to menopause, and what works for one person may not work for another. It is always best to consult with a healthcare provider before making any significant changes to your diet or lifestyle.

Benefits of Superfoods for Menopause

Menopause is a natural biological process that marks the end of a woman's reproductive years. During this time, the body undergoes significant hormonal changes, which can lead to various physical and emotional symptoms. While menopause is a natural process, some women experience severe symptoms that affect their quality of life. Eating a healthy, balanced diet is an important part of managing menopause symptoms, and incorporating superfoods into your diet can provide additional benefits.

Here are some of the benefits of superfoods for menopause and how they can help alleviate some of the symptoms associated with this transition:

Soy Products:

Soy products are one of the most well-known superfoods for menopause. Soy contains compounds called isoflavones, which are phytoestrogens that mimic the effects of estrogen in the body. These compounds can help reduce the severity of hot flashes and night sweats, two common symptoms of menopause.

One study conducted in 2012 found that women who consumed soy isoflavones had a 21% reduction in hot flash frequency compared to those who consumed a placebo. Another study found that soy isoflavones may help reduce bone loss and improve bone density, which is particularly important for women going through menopause.

Flaxseeds:

Flaxseeds are another superfood that can benefit menopausal women. Flaxseeds are high in lignans, a type of phytoestrogen that may help regulate hormone levels in menopausal women. This can help reduce the severity of symptoms like hot flashes, mood swings, and vaginal dryness.

Flaxseeds are also an excellent source of omega-3 fatty acids, which can help reduce inflammation in the body. Inflammation is a key factor in many chronic diseases, including heart disease, diabetes, and cancer. Eating flaxseeds regularly may help reduce the risk of these diseases and promote overall health and wellbeing.

Leafy Greens:

Leafy greens like kale, spinach, and collard greens are packed with vitamins and minerals that can benefit menopausal women. They are particularly high in calcium, a mineral that is important for maintaining strong bones.

As women age and go through menopause, their risk of osteoporosis (a condition characterized by weak, brittle bones) increases. Eating a diet rich in calcium can help reduce the risk of this condition and promote bone health. Leafy greens are also high in antioxidants, which can help reduce inflammation and promote overall health.

Berries:

Berries like blueberries, strawberries, and raspberries are loaded with antioxidants that can help reduce oxidative stress in the body. Oxidative stress occurs when there is an imbalance between the production of free radicals (molecules that can damage cells) and the body's ability to neutralize them.

Oxidative stress has been linked to many chronic diseases, including cancer, heart disease, and Alzheimer's disease. Eating a diet rich in antioxidants can help reduce the risk of these diseases and promote overall health.

Berries are also high in fiber, which can help regulate digestion and reduce the risk of heart disease. They are a great snack option for women going through menopause who may be experiencing digestive issues or looking for a healthy alternative to sugary snacks.

Fatty Fish:

Fatty fish like salmon, tuna, and sardines are loaded with omega-3 fatty acids, a type of healthy fat that can benefit menopausal women in many ways. Omega-3 fatty acids have been shown to help reduce inflammation in the body, which can reduce the risk of chronic diseases like heart disease and cancer.

Omega-3 fatty acids may also help improve cognitive function and reduce the risk of depression. Depression is a common symptom of menopause, and incorporating fatty fish into your diet may.

Nuts:

Nuts like almonds, walnuts, and pistachios are high in healthy fats, protein, and fiber, making them an excellent snack option for menopausal women. Nuts are also a good source of vitamin E, an antioxidant that can help reduce oxidative stress in the body.

One study found that women who consumed more nuts had a lower risk of heart disease, diabetes, and cancer. Eating a handful of nuts each day can help reduce the risk of these diseases and promote overall health.

Avocado:

Avocado is a unique fruit that is high in healthy fats and fiber. It is also a good source of potassium, a mineral that is important for maintaining healthy blood pressure levels.

Menopausal women are at an increased risk of developing high blood pressure, and eating a diet rich in potassium can help reduce this risk. Avocado is also high in vitamin K, a nutrient that is important for bone health.

Turmeric:

Turmeric is a spice that has been used for centuries in traditional medicine. It is high in a compound called curcumin, which has anti-inflammatory and antioxidant properties.

One study found that women who took a curcumin supplement experienced a reduction in hot flashes and night sweats. Turmeric can also help reduce inflammation in the body and promote overall health.

Greek Yogurt:

Greek yogurt is high in protein and calcium, making it an excellent snack option for menopausal women. Calcium is important for maintaining strong bones, and consuming enough protein can help preserve muscle mass as women age.

Greek yogurt is also high in probiotics, which can help improve gut health and boost the immune system. As women age, their immune system can weaken, so incorporating probiotics into their diet can help support overall health.

Cruciferous Vegetables:

Cruciferous vegetables like broccoli, cauliflower, and Brussels sprouts are high in fiber, vitamins, and minerals that can benefit menopausal women. They are particularly high in vitamin C, a nutrient that can help boost the immune system and reduce the risk of chronic diseases.

Cruciferous vegetables are also high in sulforaphane, a compound that has been shown to have anti-cancer properties. Eating a diet rich in cruciferous vegetables can help reduce the risk of cancer and promote overall health.

CHAPTER FOUR

Exercise for Menopause

Menopause is a natural biological process that marks the end of a woman's reproductive life. It typically occurs between the ages of 45 and 55 and is characterized by the cessation of menstrual periods. During this time, many women experience a variety of physical and emotional changes, including hot flashes, night sweats, mood swings, and weight gain. Exercise is an important component of managing menopause symptoms and maintaining overall health.

Regular physical activity has been shown to help manage menopause symptoms, including hot flashes, mood swings, and sleep disturbances. Exercise can also help maintain bone density, which is important as women's estrogen levels decrease during menopause, putting them at greater risk for osteoporosis. Additionally, exercise can help control weight gain, which is another common symptom of menopause.

There are many types of exercise that can be beneficial for menopausal women, including aerobic exercise, strength training, and flexibility exercises.

Aerobic exercise, such as brisk walking, jogging, cycling, or swimming, can improve cardiovascular health and reduce the risk of heart disease, which is a leading cause of death among women. Additionally, aerobic exercise has been shown to reduce hot flashes and improve mood and sleep quality.

Strength training, such as lifting weights or using resistance bands, can help maintain muscle mass and bone density, which can decline with age and hormonal changes. Strength training can also improve balance and reduce the risk of falls, which is important as women age.

Flexibility exercises, such as yoga or stretching, can improve range of motion and reduce muscle stiffness, which can be beneficial for women experiencing joint pain or stiffness during menopause.

It is important to start slowly and gradually increase the intensity and duration of exercise as tolerated. Women who have not been physically active in some time may want to start with low-impact activities, such as walking or swimming, before progressing to higher-impact activities, such as running or aerobics.

In addition to the physical benefits, exercise can also have psychological benefits for menopausal women. Regular physical activity has been shown to improve mood, reduce stress, and improve overall quality of life.

Women who are experiencing menopause should talk to their healthcare provider before starting a new exercise program, particularly if they have any underlying health conditions or concerns.

In conclusion, regular exercise is an important component of managing menopause symptoms and maintaining overall health. Women should aim for a combination of aerobic exercise, strength training, and flexibility exercises to achieve the maximum benefits.

It is important to start slowly and gradually increase the intensity and duration of exercise as tolerated. Women should also talk to their healthcare provider before starting a new exercise program.

Stress Management for Menopause

Menopause is a natural transition that every woman goes through at some point in her life. However, the hormonal changes and physical symptoms that accompany menopause can often lead to stress and anxiety. Stress management techniques can help women navigate this time with greater ease and improve their overall quality of life.

1. Exercise

Exercise is a powerful stress buster. Physical activity helps to release endorphins, which are natural feel-good chemicals in the brain. Exercise also helps to reduce muscle tension and improve sleep quality. Women going through menopause should aim for at least 30 minutes of moderate physical activity most days of the week. This can include activities such as walking, jogging, swimming, or yoga.

2. Mind-Body Practices

Mind-body practices, such as meditation, deep breathing, and yoga, are effective ways to manage stress. These practices help to calm the mind and relax the body, reducing feelings of anxiety and tension. Women can benefit from incorporating these practices into their daily routine, either in the morning or before bed.

3. Cognitive Behavioral Therapy (CBT)

Cognitive behavioral therapy (CBT) is a form of talk therapy that focuses on changing negative thought patterns and behaviors. CBT can help women identify and challenge negative thought patterns and develop new coping strategies to manage stress. It has been shown to be effective in reducing symptoms of anxiety and depression in women going through menopause.

4. Relaxation Techniques

Relaxation techniques, such as progressive muscle relaxation or guided imagery, can help women to relax their muscles and calm their minds. These techniques involve focusing on different parts of the body and consciously relaxing them. Guided imagery involves visualizing a peaceful scene or environment to promote relaxation.

5. Acupuncture

Acupuncture involves inserting thin needles into specific points on the body. This practice is based on the belief that energy flows through the body along specific pathways, and that by stimulating these pathways, balance can be restored. Acupuncture has been shown to be effective in reducing symptoms of hot flashes, sleep disturbances, and anxiety in menopausal women.

6. Herbal Remedies

Herbal remedies, such as black cohosh, evening primrose oil, and dong quai, are often used to manage menopause symptoms. However, it is important to consult with a healthcare provider before using any herbal remedy, as they can have potential side effects and interactions with other medications.

7. Social Support

Social support is an important aspect of stress management. Women going through menopause can benefit from connecting with others who are experiencing similar challenges. This can be through support groups, online forums, or simply talking to friends and family members. Sharing experiences and receiving emotional support can help women feel less isolated and better equipped to manage stress.

8. Healthy Lifestyle Habits

Maintaining healthy lifestyle habits, such as getting enough sleep, eating a balanced diet, and limiting alcohol and caffeine, can help women to manage stress and improve their overall well-being. Women should aim for 7-8 hours of sleep per night, eat a diet rich in fruits, vegetables, whole grains, and lean protein, and limit alcohol and caffeine intake.

In conclusion, managing stress is an important component of navigating menopause with greater ease. Women going through menopause can benefit from incorporating stress management techniques into their daily routine, such as exercise, mind-body practices, cognitive behavioral therapy, relaxation techniques, acupuncture, herbal remedies, social support, and healthy lifestyle habits.

It is important to consult with a healthcare provider before starting any new treatment or herbal remedy. With the right tools and support, women can manage stress and enjoy a healthy and fulfilling life during menopause.

Sleep Hygiene for Menopause

Menopause is a natural biological process that marks the end of a woman's reproductive years. One of the common symptoms of menopause is sleep disturbances, including difficulty falling asleep, staying asleep, and waking up feeling unrefreshed. Fortunately, there are several sleep hygiene practices that women can adopt to improve the quality of their sleep during menopause.

1. Stick to a regular sleep schedule

Establishing a regular sleep schedule is crucial for promoting healthy sleep during menopause. Going to bed and waking up at the same time every day helps to regulate the body's circadian rhythm and promote better sleep quality. Women should aim for seven to eight hours of sleep per night and avoid oversleeping, which can lead to feeling groggy and less alert.

2. Create a comfortable sleep environment

Creating a comfortable sleep environment is essential for promoting quality sleep. The bedroom should be quiet, cool, and dark. Women should invest in a comfortable mattress, pillows, and bedding to enhance their sleep comfort. It is also important to minimize noise and light disruptions, such as using blackout curtains and earplugs.

3. Avoid stimulating activities before bedtime

Engaging in stimulating activities before bedtime can make it harder to fall asleep. Women should avoid using electronic devices, such as smartphones and laptops, for at least an hour before bedtime. The blue light emitted by electronic devices can interfere with the body's natural sleep-wake cycle. Instead, women can engage in relaxing activities before bedtime, such as reading a book or taking a warm bath.

4. Limit caffeine and alcohol intake

Caffeine and alcohol consumption can disrupt sleep during menopause. Women should limit their caffeine intake and avoid consuming it after lunchtime. Alcohol consumption may lead to initial drowsiness, but it can interfere with the body's natural sleep cycle and lead to poor sleep quality.

5. Engage in regular exercise

Regular exercise has been shown to improve sleep quality during menopause. Women should aim for at least 30 minutes of moderate-intensity exercise most days of the week. However, it is important to avoid exercising close to bedtime, as it can increase alertness and make it harder to fall asleep.

6. Manage hot flashes

Hot flashes are a common symptom of menopause and can disrupt sleep. Women can manage hot flashes by wearing breathable clothing and keeping the bedroom cool. They can also use cooling products, such as fans, cooling pillows, and cooling sheets, to reduce the intensity and frequency of hot flashes.

7. Practice relaxation techniques

Practicing relaxation techniques, such as deep breathing, meditation, and progressive muscle relaxation, can help women to reduce stress and promote sleep. These techniques help to calm the mind and relax the body, promoting a restful night's sleep.

In conclusion, sleep disturbances are a common symptom of menopause, but adopting good sleep hygiene practices can help women to improve their sleep quality. Women should aim for a regular sleep schedule, create a comfortable sleep environment, avoid stimulating activities before bedtime, limit caffeine and alcohol intake, engage in regular exercise, manage hot flashes, and practice relaxation techniques. By implementing these practices, women can improve their sleep quality and enjoy a more restful night's sleep.

8. Consider hormone therapy

Hormone therapy, also known as hormone replacement therapy, can help to relieve menopausal symptoms, including sleep disturbances. Hormone therapy involves taking estrogen and progesterone supplements to replace the hormones that the body no longer produces. However, it is important to discuss the risks and benefits of hormone therapy with a healthcare provider before starting this treatment.

9. Keep a sleep diary

Keeping a sleep diary can help women to identify patterns and habits that may be disrupting their sleep. Women can use the diary to track their bedtime, wake time, and sleep quality, as well as any factors that may be affecting their sleep, such as caffeine intake or exercise habits. By identifying these factors, women can make changes to their sleep hygiene habits and improve their sleep quality.

10. Avoid napping

Napping during the day can disrupt the body's natural sleep-wake cycle and make it harder to fall asleep at night. Women should try to avoid napping during the day or limit it to no more than 20 minutes.

11. Seek treatment for underlying conditions

Underlying medical conditions, such as sleep apnea or restless leg syndrome, can disrupt sleep during menopause. Women should seek treatment for these conditions to improve their sleep quality.

12. Use relaxation techniques

Relaxation techniques, such as yoga and tai chi, can help women to reduce stress and promote sleep. These techniques promote relaxation and improve the body's natural sleep-wake cycle.

13. Consider natural remedies

Some women may find relief from menopausal symptoms, including sleep disturbances, by using natural remedies. These remedies include herbal supplements, such as valerian root and chamomile tea, which have been shown to promote relaxation and improve sleep quality. However, it is important to discuss the use of these remedies with a healthcare provider before starting them, as they may interact with other medications or have unwanted side effects.

By adopting these sleep hygiene practices, women can improve their sleep quality during menopause and reduce the impact of sleep disturbances on their daily lives.

It is important to note that women may need to experiment with different practices to find the combination that works best for them. Women should also consult with their healthcare provider if sleep disturbances persist or interfere with their daily activities.

Chapter five

Menopause Supplements and Medications

Menopause is a natural stage in a woman's life when her menstrual periods stop permanently, typically occurring around age 50. During menopause, women may experience a variety of symptoms, including hot flashes, night sweats, mood swings, vaginal dryness, and decreased libido. While hormone replacement therapy (HRT) can help alleviate some of these symptoms, many women prefer to use supplements to manage their menopause symptoms.

Here are some common supplements that may help alleviate menopause symptoms:

- **Black cohosh:** This herbal supplement has been shown to reduce hot flashes and improve mood in some women.

- **Soy isoflavones**: Soy contains plant-based estrogens called phytoestrogens, which may help alleviate hot flashes and other symptoms of menopause.
- **Flaxseed:** Flaxseed contains lignans, which are also plant-based estrogens. Consuming flaxseed may help reduce hot flashes and improve vaginal dryness.
- **Vitamin D**: Women going through menopause may be at risk for vitamin D deficiency, which can lead to bone loss. Taking a vitamin D supplement may help improve bone health.
- **Calcium**: Women going through menopause may also be at risk for osteoporosis, so taking a calcium **Magnesium**: This mineral can help reduce hot flashes and improve sleep quality, which is often disrupted during menopause.
- **Evening primrose oil:** This supplement contains gamma-linolenic acid (GLA), which can help alleviate hot flashes and other menopause symptoms.
- **St. John's wort:** This herbal supplement may help improve mood and reduce anxiety, which can be common during menopause.

- **Red clover:** This herb contains phytoestrogens, which can help alleviate hot flashes and other menopause symptoms.
- **Vitamin E:** Some studies have shown that vitamin E may help reduce hot flashes in menopausal women.

It's important to remember that supplements are not regulated by the FDA, and their safety and effectiveness can vary. It's important to purchase supplements from reputable sources, and to talk to your healthcare provider before starting any new supplements, especially if you are taking other medications or have any underlying health conditions. Additionally, supplements should not be used as a replacement for medical treatment or advice.

- **Hormone Replacement Therapy**

Hormone replacement therapy (HRT) is a treatment that involves supplementing the body with hormones that it is no longer producing in sufficient amounts due to menopause. HRT can help alleviate some of the symptoms of menopause, including hot flashes, night sweats, vaginal dryness, and mood swings.

- **There are two main types of HRT:** estrogen-only therapy and combination therapy (estrogen and progesterone). Estrogen-only therapy is typically prescribed to women who have had a hysterectomy (surgical removal of the uterus), while combination therapy is prescribed to women who still have their uterus. Progesterone is added to the estrogen in combination therapy to help protect the uterus from cancer.

HRT can be administered in a variety of forms, including pills, patches, gels, creams, and vaginal rings. The type of HRT and the dosage will depend on a woman's individual symptoms and medical history.

While HRT can be effective in alleviating menopause symptoms, it is not without risks. Long-term use of HRT has been associated with an increased risk of breast cancer, heart disease, stroke, and blood clots. Women who are considering HRT should discuss the risks and benefits with their healthcare provider and choose the lowest effective dose for the shortest duration necessary to manage their symptoms.

It's important to note that HRT is not suitable for everyone, and there are some medical conditions, such as certain types of cancer and blood clots, that may make HRT unsafe. Additionally, women who have a history of breast cancer, heart disease, or stroke should discuss the risks and benefits of HRT with their healthcare provider before starting treatment.

Other Medications for Menopause Symptoms

In addition to hormone replacement therapy and supplements, there are other medications that can be used to manage menopause symptoms. Here are some examples:

- **Antidepressants**: Selective serotonin reuptake inhibitors (SSRIs) and serotonin-norepinephrine reuptake inhibitors (SNRIs) are commonly used to treat hot flashes and night sweats. These medications work by regulating the levels of serotonin and norepinephrine in the brain, which can help reduce the frequency and severity of hot flashes.

- **Gabapentin**: This medication is typically used to treat seizures and nerve pain, but it can also be effective in reducing hot flashes.
- **Clonidine**: This medication is typically used to treat high blood pressure, but it can also help reduce hot flashes and improve sleep quality in menopausal women.
- **Vaginal estrogen**: For women who experience vaginal dryness and discomfort during sex, vaginal estrogen cream, tablet, or ring can be used to restore moisture and elasticity to the vaginal tissue.

It's important to note that like any medication, these drugs can have side effects and risks, and they should only be used under the guidance of a healthcare provider. Women should discuss the risks and benefits of these medications with their healthcare provider and choose the treatment that is best for their individual needs and medical history. Additionally, lifestyle changes, such as maintaining a healthy weight, exercising regularly, and reducing stress, can also help manage menopause symptoms.

CHAPTER SIX

Managing Menopause Symptoms Naturally

Menopause is a natural process that every woman experiences as they age. During menopause, a woman's body goes through several hormonal changes, leading to several uncomfortable symptoms like hot flashes, night sweats, mood swings, and insomnia.

While there are several prescription medications available to treat these symptoms, many women prefer natural remedies to avoid potential side effects. Here are some herbal remedies that may help alleviate menopause symptoms:

- **Black Cohosh:** This herb is commonly used to relieve hot flashes, mood swings, and vaginal dryness. It works by reducing the levels of luteinizing hormone, which can cause hot flashes.

- **Red Clover**: This herb is rich in phytoestrogens, which can help balance hormone levels and reduce hot flashes and night sweats.
- **Dong Quai**: Also known as "female ginseng," this herb is often used to reduce hot flashes, vaginal dryness, and mood swings.
- **Ginseng**: This herb has been found to be useful in reducing anxiety and depression, two common symptoms of menopause.
- **St. John's Wort**: This herb is commonly used to treat depression, which can be a symptom of menopause.
- **Evening Primrose Oil**: This oil is rich in gamma-linolenic acid (GLA), which can help reduce hot flashes, mood swings, and vaginal dryness.

It is essential to speak to a healthcare professional before taking any herbal remedies, especially if you have underlying medical conditions or are taking other medications. Some herbs can interact with prescription drugs or exacerbate certain medical conditions, so it's crucial to use caution when incorporating them into your health regimen.

- **Flaxseed:** Flaxseed is high in lignans, which can help balance hormone levels and reduce hot flashes.
- **Chasteberry**: This herb is commonly used to alleviate mood swings and irritability during menopause.
- **Sage**: Sage is an excellent herb for reducing hot flashes and night sweats, and it can also improve mood and cognitive function.
- **Licorice**: Licorice root can help balance hormone levels and reduce hot flashes and other menopause symptoms.

Ashwagandha: Ashwagandha is an adaptogenic herb that can help reduce stress and anxiety, which are common during menopause.

- **Maca**: Maca root is often used to boost energy, improve mood, and reduce hot flashes.

It's important to note that herbal remedies are not regulated by the FDA, so the quality and purity of these products may vary. Always purchase herbs from reputable sources, and follow the recommended dosages carefully. Also, it's essential to continue to see a healthcare professional for regular check-ups and to monitor any potential health risks associated with menopause.

Acupuncture for Menopause Symptoms

Acupuncture is a traditional Chinese medicine technique that involves inserting thin needles into specific points on the body to stimulate the flow of energy, or qi. Acupuncture has been used for centuries to treat various health conditions, including menopause symptoms. Here are some ways that acupuncture may help alleviate menopause symptoms:

Reducing hot flashes: Acupuncture has been found to be effective in reducing the frequency and severity of hot flashes, which are one of the most common symptoms of menopause.

Improving sleep: Menopause can disrupt sleep patterns, and acupuncture can help improve the quality and quantity of sleep.

Reducing anxiety and depression: Menopause can cause mood swings, anxiety, and depression, and acupuncture can help reduce these symptoms by promoting relaxation and reducing stress.

Alleviating vaginal dryness: Acupuncture can help stimulate blood flow to the vaginal area, reducing dryness and discomfort.

Balancing hormones: Acupuncture can help balance hormone levels in the body, which can help alleviate many menopause symptoms.

Acupuncture is generally considered safe when performed by a licensed and trained practitioner. However, some people may experience mild side effects such as bruising, soreness, or bleeding at the needle insertion site. It's essential to speak to a healthcare professional before trying acupuncture, especially if you have underlying medical conditions or are taking other medications. Additionally, acupuncture may not be effective for everyone, and some people may require several sessions to experience significant relief.

Other Natural Approaches to Menopause Symptoms

In addition to herbal remedies and acupuncture, there are several other natural approaches that may help alleviate menopause symptoms. Here are some of them:

Exercise: Regular exercise can help reduce hot flashes, improve mood, and promote better sleep.

Healthy diet: A diet rich in whole grains, fruits, vegetables, and lean proteins can help reduce menopause symptoms. Avoiding spicy foods, alcohol, and caffeine may also help reduce hot flashes.

Stress management: Stress can exacerbate menopause symptoms, so practicing relaxation techniques such as meditation, yoga, or deep breathing exercises can help reduce stress and promote relaxation.

Supplements: Some supplements like calcium, vitamin D, and magnesium may help reduce the risk of osteoporosis, which is a common concern during menopause.

Acupressure: Acupressure is a technique that involves applying pressure to specific points on the body to relieve symptoms. It can be done at home or with the help of a trained practitioner.

Cognitive-behavioral therapy (CBT): CBT is a type of therapy that can help women manage mood swings, anxiety, and depression during menopause by teaching them coping skills and cognitive restructuring techniques.

It's essential to speak to a healthcare professional before trying any new approach, including natural remedies, to manage menopause symptoms. They can help determine the most effective and safe options based on your individual health history and current symptoms.

Mind-body techniques: Mind-body techniques such as biofeedback, hypnotherapy, and guided imagery can help reduce stress, promote relaxation, and improve overall well-being.

Essential oils: Some essential oils such as lavender, peppermint, and clary sage may help reduce hot flashes, improve sleep, and promote relaxation.

Chiropractic care: Chiropractic care can help alleviate back pain, which is a common complaint during menopause.

Massage therapy: Massage therapy can help reduce stress, alleviate muscle tension, and improve overall well-being.

Aromatherapy: Aromatherapy involves using essential oils to promote relaxation and reduce stress. Essential oils can be used in a diffuser or added to bathwater.

Sleep hygiene: Maintaining good sleep hygiene habits, such as avoiding electronics before bed, keeping the bedroom cool and dark, and sticking to a regular sleep schedule, can help improve sleep during menopause.

It's important to note that natural remedies may not work for everyone, and some may require several weeks or months of consistent use to see results. Additionally, it's essential to speak to a healthcare professional before trying any new approach to manage menopause symptoms. They can help determine the most effective and safe options based on your individual health history and current symptoms.

CONCLUSION

The Importance of a Menopause Diet Plan

A menopause diet plan is essential for women as they enter this stage of life. Menopause is a natural biological process that occurs in women when they stop menstruating, and it marks the end of reproductive life. As a result, women's bodies undergo significant changes during this phase, including hormonal fluctuations that can lead to weight gain, bone loss, and an increased risk of certain diseases.

A healthy menopause diet plan can help women manage the symptoms and health risks associated with this stage of life. Here are some reasons why a menopause diet plan is important:

Weight management: Many women experience weight gain during menopause due to hormonal changes. A menopause diet plan can help women maintain a healthy weight by incorporating nutrient-dense foods, controlling portions, and limiting high-calorie foods.

Bone health: As women age, their bone density decreases, leading to an increased risk of osteoporosis. A menopause diet plan should include foods rich in calcium, vitamin D, and other bone-strengthening nutrients to help maintain bone health.

Heart health: Women's risk of heart disease increases after menopause due to hormonal changes. A menopause diet plan can help reduce this risk by incorporating heart-healthy foods like fruits, vegetables, whole grains, lean protein, and healthy fats.

Managing hot flashes: Hot flashes are a common symptom of menopause, and some foods and drinks can trigger them. A menopause diet plan can help women avoid these triggers and manage hot flashes more effectively.

Mood and energy: Hormonal changes during menopause can also affect women's mood and energy levels. A menopause diet plan that includes nutrient-dense foods can help stabilize mood and energy levels.

In conclusion, a menopause diet plan is essential for women's health and wellbeing during this stage of life. It can help manage symptoms and reduce the risk of certain diseases. Women should consult with their healthcare providers to develop a personalized menopause diet plan that meets their individual needs and preferences.

Tips for Successful Menopause Management

Menopause is a natural and unavoidable phase of life that every woman experiences as they age. While it can be challenging for some women, there are several tips for successful menopause management that can help women navigate this transition with ease. Here are some tips:

1. **Maintain a healthy lifestyle**: Maintaining a healthy lifestyle is key to successful menopause management. This includes a balanced diet, regular exercise, and sufficient sleep. A healthy lifestyle can help manage menopause symptoms such as hot flashes, mood swings, and weight gain.
2. **Stay hydrated**: Menopause can lead to dry skin and vaginal dryness, which can be uncomfortable. Drinking plenty of water can help keep the body hydrated and alleviate these symptoms.

3. **Manage stress**: Stress can exacerbate menopause symptoms such as hot flashes and mood swings. Managing stress through techniques such as meditation, yoga, or deep breathing can help reduce symptoms and improve overall wellbeing.
4. **Consider hormone therapy**: Hormone therapy can help alleviate severe menopause symptoms such as hot flashes and vaginal dryness. Women should consult with their healthcare providers to determine if hormone therapy is right for them.
5. **Stay socially active**: Maintaining social connections can help women stay engaged and maintain their mental health during menopause. It can also provide a support network for managing symptoms.

6. **Practice self-care**: Practicing self-care can help women feel their best during menopause. This can include activities such as getting a massage, taking a relaxing bath, or reading a book.

In conclusion, successful menopause management requires a comprehensive approach that involves maintaining a healthy lifestyle, managing stress, considering hormone therapy, staying socially active, and practicing self-care. Women should consult with their healthcare providers to develop a personalized plan that meets their individual needs and preferences.

Embracing Menopause as a New Chapter in Your Life.

Menopause marks the end of reproductive life for women and can be a challenging transition. However, it can also be an opportunity for women to embrace a new chapter in their lives. Here are some ways to embrace menopause as a new chapter in your life:

Celebrate your accomplishments: Menopause can be a time to reflect on your life's accomplishments and celebrate them. Take the time to acknowledge your successes and the experiences that have made you the person you are today.

Focus on self-care: Menopause can be a time to prioritize self-care and focus on your physical and emotional wellbeing. Consider activities such as meditation, yoga, or spending time in nature.

Explore new hobbies: Menopause can be a time to explore new hobbies or interests that you may not have had time for in the past. Consider taking up a new hobby or activity that brings you joy.

Embrace your sexuality: Menopause does not have to mean the end of your sex life. Embrace your sexuality and explore new ways to enjoy intimacy with your partner or yourself.

Connect with other women: Menopause is a shared experience for women and can be an opportunity to connect with other women going through the same transition. Join a support group or attend events focused on menopause to connect with others and share your experiences.

Embrace aging: Menopause is a reminder that we are all getting older, but it does not have to be a negative experience. Embrace aging and focus on the positive aspects of growing older, such as increased wisdom and experience.

In conclusion, menopause can be a challenging transition for women, but it can also be an opportunity to embrace a new chapter in your life. By celebrating your accomplishments, focusing on self-care, exploring new hobbies, embracing your sexuality, connecting with other women, and embracing aging, you can make the most of this new phase of life.

Printed in Great Britain
by Amazon